A Better Way: Real Talk with Real People

A Better Way
Real Talk with Real People
Facilitator's Handbook

Copyright © 2020
Linda H. Williams

Cover Design Concept By:
Tia Jones

All Rights Reserved.
No portion of this publication may be reproduced, stored in an electronic system, or transmitted in any form or by any means (electronic, mechanical, photocopy, recording, or otherwise) without written permission from the author or publisher. Brief quotations may be used in literary reviews.

Facilitator's Handbook ISBN 13: 978-1-948853-00-2
Client's Workbook ISBN 13: 978-1-948853-01-9

The content provided within this book is for general informational purposes only. The methods shared are done so by the author and are not intended to be a definitive set of instructions for the reader's life. By continuing, you acknowledge you are responsible for any use of this material and will not hold the author or publisher liable for any legal recourses under any circumstance.

For more information and bulk ordering details, contact:
Pearly Gates Publishing, LLC
Angela Edwards, CEO
P.O. Box 62287
Houston, TX 77205
BestSeller@PearlyGatesPublishing.com

A Better Way: Real Talk with Real People

What People Are Saying About This Course

"This class is one of my favorites. It helps me to identify my strengths and weaknesses. It also helps me to learn how to deal with building myself up, staying true to myself, and owning both my good and bad. Thank you so much!"
~ M.B. ~

"I enjoy the open dialogue. Before I have a chance to rebut with a question, it is already answered. I call this class 'A Healthy Self-Evaluation.'"
~ K.B. ~

"This was an informative class. I enjoyed the talk with Ms. Linda. I've learned that I must take a hard look at myself in order to make changes for a better tomorrow for my family and me."
~ D.M. ~

"I personally think the class can be helpful in the long run for those who really want to change. It's called "Real Talk," so being able to be "real" and "understood" can change a person for the better — mentally and physically."
~ Anonymous ~

"I love this class! It's very informative and teaches you to do a self-evaluation. I learned I need to look at myself to see where my problem lies."
~ V.D. ~

"I found your class to be straightforward toward the issues that are sometimes hard to discuss in an open group. I feel like I have a better sense of self."
~ B.B. ~

"Well-needed class. Right on time. Very understanding."
~ Anonymous ~

"This class made me look at things in other ways. I've been going through so much, and this made me realize things differently. You are amazing! Much love. Thank you deeply!"
~ Anonymous ~

A Better Way: Real Talk with Real People

"I like this class because everything you talk about really hit me and made me think about all the things I've been through in my life. I want a better life for myself and don't want to keep making the same mistakes. This class really helps me. Thank you!"
~ **Anonymous** ~

"This class is very uplifting and powerful. It makes me feel good about myself after attending. Thank you!"
~ **Anonymous** ~

"I think this class was very good. The instructor made some very good points on better ways of looking at life. Thank you very much!"
~ **Anonymous** ~

"I love the class – point-blank! It is very rewarding and uplifting. Keep it coming!"
~ **A.H.** ~

"I'm grateful for this class. It's very insightful."
~ **K.D.** ~

"I enjoyed this class. I gained more wisdom on becoming a better person."
~ **B.T.** ~

"I really needed this class. I have been looking for better ways to live for a long time. I don't have many people to talk to about my problems or who would listen to me, but this class gave me some enlightenment. Thank you!"
~ **Anonymous** ~

"I think this class was wonderful and much-needed. It allows you to open up and admit the improper decisions you have made in life. I was able to hear other men who have been through similar situations I have experienced. Overall, it helped me with processing my life as a whole. Thank you!"
~ **J.L.** ~

Dedication

This project is dedicated to my sons
— my legacy —
Emory and Raphael.

This project is also dedicated to my parents
— my history —
Rev. & Mrs. John T. Hilliard.

A Better Way: Real Talk with Real People

Introduction

What is Cognitive Behavioral Therapy?

A Better Way: Real Talk with Real People is based on Cognitive Behavioral Therapy practices. Cognitive Behavior Therapy (CBT) is a short-term, goal-oriented psychotherapy treatment that takes a hands-on, practical approach to problem-solving. Its goal is to change patterns of thinking or behavior that are behind people's difficulties, and so change the way they feel.

How does CBT work?

CBT is most often used in cases of anxiety, depression, and worry. However, it is also quite effective in identifying the underlying reason why people make specific choices in life. Often, people deal with the trigger and the action resulting from it without addressing the trigger itself.

Since every action begins with a thought, this workbook serves as a curriculum for anyone in the business of helping themselves and/or others. CBT works by looking at how we think and how our thinking is based on our emotions and subsequent behavior. There is a direct correlation between our emotions and our thoughts. We don't always have control over the situation, circumstance, or other people, but we do have control over how we respond. A large part of how we respond is a direct result of our thoughts regarding the situation.

This course will help the client identify and analyze their thoughts to distinguish between healthy and unhealthy thought patterns. Once they identify what those are and why they have them, they can begin to work to replace them with healthy, constructive thoughts. The thoughts will not be merely a "passing fancy," but rather realistic thoughts based on sound logic and reasoning. Eventually, unhealthy thoughts will become less prevalent, which would ideally improve their actions and lead to a better quality of life.

A Better Way: Real Talk with Real People

This 12-week course requires **input** from the facilitator and a **commitment** from the client to participate in the weekly exercises. Although this is a short-term treatment, the client must be willing to work outside of the class instruction to complete the associated weekly worksheets and begin to apply the lessons to their daily lives. At the completion of this course, the client will have a better understanding of themselves, along with being better equipped to delve into their own motives.

As one client stated, *"I came to this class to learn to have more willpower and be quick to recognize my triggers before I act. The instructor made some very good points on better ways of looking at life and how I need to be in better control of my thoughts."*

A Better Way: Real Talk with Real People

Table of Contents

What People Are Saying About This Course 4

Dedication 6

Introduction 7

Week 1 – Prisons 10

Week 2 – Happy vs. Unhappy 16

Week 3 – Baggage: Anger 25

Week 4 – Controlling Your Life 32

Week 5 – Forgiveness 43

Week 6 – Toxic Relationships 49

Week 7 – Guilt 56

Week 8 – Controlling Your Thoughts 65

Week 9 – Disappointment 74

Week 10 – Choices 81

Week 11 – Dishonesty 87

Week 12 – Goal Setting 96

A Better Way: Real Talk with Real People
Week 1 – Prisons

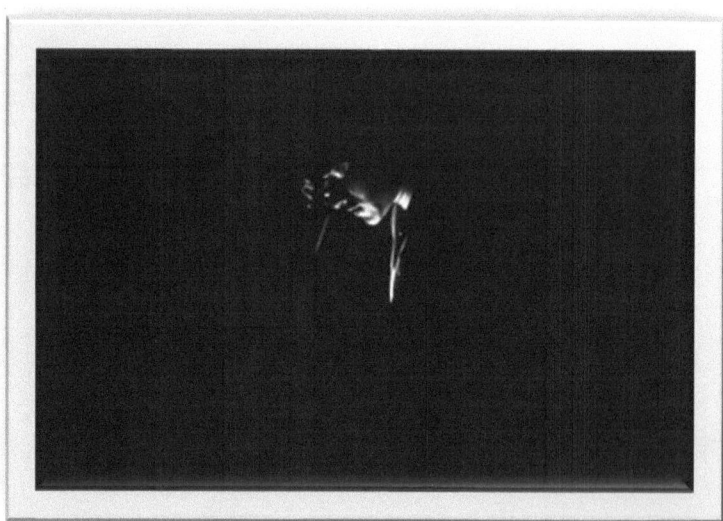

1. **INTRODUCTION:** The facilitator introduces himself/herself and states the purpose of the class.
   "The purpose of this class is to provide you with the tools to modify behavior by changing your thought pattern. Every action begins with a thought. Today, let's talk about prisons – not the one with bars."

2. **GROUP DISCUSSION:** Name some situations in life that can be thought of as a prison.
   Facilitator, provide a personal response (i.e., an abusive relationship, poverty, debt, substance abuse, other types of addictions).

_____
_____
_____
_____

3. **TYPES OF PRISONS:**
   a. **The Blame Game** – The 'Blame Game' consists of blaming another person for an event or state of affairs that is undesirable and persisting in it, instead of proactively making changes that will make the situation better.

The situation: You think it is other people's fault that you have certain negative feelings or experiences.

The example: *"It is my ex's fault that I can't maintain relationships"* or *"My parents have caused all my problems."* Then, *"It is **their** fault I'm in this situation."*

The solution: Recognize it is not useful to blame others. It doesn't move you forward. You must have accountability and take responsibility for yourself.

GROUP DISCUSSION: What happens when you blame other people? Facilitator, provide a personal response.

_____
_____
_____
_____

Often, removing blame requires forgiveness. When you hold onto anger, you are poisoning yourself. Anger does not undo what happened. The person or situation you are angry about is often unaffected. The most important person we must forgive is ourselves. Before that can be done, we must accept a certain amount of responsibility.

Even if something happened that was not your fault, you must determine what you can do to contribute to solving the problem. You are the only person who can change your situation.

A Better Way: Real Talk with Real People

GROUP DISCUSSION: Why do you think people often have a low opinion of themselves?

Facilitator, provide a personal response.

_____
_____
_____
_____
_____
_____
_____
_____
_____

Let's look at some reasons why:

a. **Self-Love:** You would think that self-love is a natural process. However, a life filled with emotional "baggage," one fraught with habitual behaviors that damage the mental and physical self, and everyday stressors can make many people feel unworthy of love within themselves. It is difficult to truly feel and express love for others if we are unable to feel and express it to ourselves first.

GROUP DISCUSSION: Why do you think people have such a hard time loving themselves?

Facilitator, provide a personal response.

_____
_____
_____
_____
_____
_____
_____

b. **We tend to pay more attention to negative experiences than positive ones.** Have you ever wondered why it's easier to remember the negative stuff? If we listen to our thoughts, we might be surprised to see how much we dwell on the negative rather than the positive. Why do you think this is so?
   GROUP DISCUSSION: Ask participants to name one negative thing that has happened in their life. Then, ask them to name one positive thing in their life. Facilitator, provide a personal response.

   _____
   _____
   _____
   _____
   _____
   _____
   _____

c. **We don't trust ourselves:** We seek ways to build our "esteem" in the world — to feel better about ourselves by being better than someone else, finding the right person to build us up, or becoming or doing what someone else wants us to do so that we feel worthy of love. Each of those paths to "self-esteem" will ultimately fail, for they are built on a system of self-doubt. Instead, we must learn to trust ourselves, to listen for, hear, and trust the whispers within that show us our true value and worth, to release the opinion and voices of others, and to trust a greater Source.
   GROUP DISCUSSION: Why do you think people will believe someone else's opinion of them?
   Facilitator, provide a personal response.

   _____
   _____
   _____
   _____
   _____
   _____

d. **Believing that nothing will ever change:** Once a person finds purpose and experiences self-love, it becomes easier to believe that tomorrow does not have to look like today. The one factor that continues to hold people back is *FEAR*—fear of the unknown and fear of failure. We begin to realize that success is rarely achieved in a straight-line pattern. Failure helps us refine our approach and takes success to a higher level. This new attitude forces us to change the question from, *"Is change possible?"* to *"How far do we desire this change to take us?"*

    GROUP DISCUSSION: What does fear mean to you? How does fear contribute to your decisions?

    Facilitator, provide a personal response.

    _____
    _____
    _____
    _____
    _____
    _____

e. **Toxic relationships:** We all know at least one person who just can't seem to let go of people in their lives who take advantage of them and, sometimes, even abuse them. Hopefully, the person being abused isn't you. What makes it even more difficult is when it is a family member. Anyone who is toxic to our physical and mental well-being should be removed from our lives. To do otherwise is to imprison ourselves.

    GROUP DISCUSSION: Give me an example of how a bad relationship can affect how you think.

    Facilitator, provide a personal response (i.e., an angry, unhappy boss).

    _____
    _____
    _____
    _____
    _____
    _____

f. Compromised core values: A core value is defined as a belief or conviction that guides and directs your behavior. We must live and act in harmony with our core values, but we can't do that if we don't know what they are. This is an area we often pay little attention to, which often leads to some self-sabotaging tendencies.

The best way to avoid this internal prison is to analyze your deepest core values and ensure that everything you do is in harmony with them.

GROUP DISCUSSION: Let's look at some core values and rank their importance. Facilitator, write on a whiteboard or easel (if available).

- Dependability
- Positivity
- Respect
- Courage
- Reliability
- Loyalty
- Commitment
- Consistency
- Honesty
- Compassion

Closing Statement: Personal prisons are related to our behavior and state of mind. They can include limiting habits and debilitating emotions, fears, and beliefs. Those obstacles prevent us from moving forward towards the attainment of our goals and objectives because of the thoughts we tend to dwell upon daily. Those thoughts naturally prevent us from making effective decisions and undertaking the actions that will help us create the momentum we need to get to our final destination.

Facilitator, distribute comment cards, and have each class member write one thing they gained from this class.

A Better Way: Real Talk with Real People
Week 2 – Happy vs. Unhappy

1. Begin class with a discussion from Week 1 – Prisons. Allow a short question-answer period.
   GROUP DISCUSSION: What is your definition of happiness? What makes people happy?
   Facilitator, provide a personal response.

   _____
   _____
   _____
   _____

2. Happiness is defined as a feeling that comes over you when you know life is good, and you can't help but smile. It is the opposite of sadness. Happiness is a sense of well-being, joy, or contentment. When people are successful, safe, or blessed, they feel happiness.

A Better Way: Real Talk with Real People

3. **What makes us happy?**
    a. **Close relationships:** The happiest people spend time with those they love, including family, partners, or friends. Intimacy with others fulfills two basic human needs: the need for social connections with others and the need for personal growth, which makes us feel fully alive.
    GROUP DISCUSSION: Who makes a person happy when they spend time with them? Why?
    Facilitator, provide a personal response.

    _____
    _____
    _____
    _____

    b. **Meaningful work:** We are happiest when engaged in activities that make us forget ourselves and lose track of time. This can be achieved when we do something we love to do. It could be making music, gardening, playing with children, practicing sports, or journaling. We experience a sense of fulfillment when using and developing our skills, talents, and abilities.
    GROUP DISCUSSION: Name an activity that could make a person feel good. Why do you think it makes them feel good?
    Facilitator, provide a personal response.

    _____
    _____
    _____
    _____

    c. **Positive thinking:** One contributing factor to happiness is a positive attitude. Be content that the house you have is "enough house," instead of envying your neighbor's bigger house. If you really must compare, compare down, and not up. For example, Olympic bronze medalists who consider themselves lucky to get a medal are happier than silver medalists who feel they missed the mark in obtaining the gold medal.

A Better Way: Real Talk with Real People

GROUP DISCUSSION: How can a person have a more positive attitude about life?

Facilitator, provide a personal response.

_____
_____
_____
_____

d. **Gratitude:** Grateful people are happy people. It doesn't matter if your glass is half-full or half-empty. What's important is that you have a glass with something in it! We focus more on what we don't have instead of what we do have.

   GROUP DISCUSSION: What does gratitude mean to you? Name something for which you are grateful.

   Facilitator, provide a personal response.

   _____
   _____
   _____
   _____

e. **Giving to others:** Many people testify that what lifted them from depression was helping others. You would be surprised by what volunteering at a homeless shelter or holding the hand of a terminally ill patient can do for you. Whatever it is, all forms of giving take us out of ourselves and set us back on the path of normalcy and happiness.

   GROUP DISCUSSION: In what ways can someone give of themselves to someone else?

   Facilitator, provide a personal response.

   _____
   _____
   _____
   _____

f. **Having a spirit of forgiveness:** Letting go of grudges and bitterness can make way for improved health and peace of mind. We often think forgiving someone means what they did was okay. Forgiveness has nothing to do with the other person. Forgiveness it purely a selfish act of freeing yourself from the emotional control of others.
GROUP DISCUSSION: What do you think are the benefits of forgiving someone?
Facilitator, provide a personal response.

_____
_____
_____
_____

Forgiveness can lead to:
- Healthier relationships
- Improved mental health
- Less anxiety, stress, and hostility
- Improved heart health
- Improved self-esteem

4. **What Makes Us Unhappy?**
   a. **Worry:** Worrying can be helpful when it spurs you to take action and solve a problem. However, if you are preoccupied with "what ifs" and worst-case-scenarios, worry becomes a problem of its own. Chronic worrying is a mental habit that can be broken. You can train your brain to remain calm and look at life from a more balanced, less fearful perspective.
   GROUP DISCUSSION: Name a problem or situation that people constantly worry about?
   Facilitator, provide a personal response.

_____
_____
_____
_____

A Better Way: Real Talk with Real People

When you begin to worry, ask yourself:

> ➤ Can I solve the problem? If so, how? If a worry pops into your head, start by asking yourself whether the problem is something you can actually solve. The following questions can help:
>
> o Is the problem something you are currently facing, rather than an imaginary "what if"?
> o If the problem is an imaginary "what if," how likely is it to happen? Is your concern realistic?
> o Can you do something about the problem or prepare for it, or is it out of your control?

b. **Thinking about all the things that could go wrong does not make life any more predictable.** You may feel safer when you are worrying, but it's just an illusion. Focusing on worst-case-scenarios will not keep bad things from happening. It will only prove to keep you from enjoying the good things you have in the present.
GROUP DISCUSSION: Let's look at a situation. Your company gets bought out by another company. What is the worst thing that could happen? Now, name one good thing in your life right now.
Facilitator, provide a personal response.

_____
_____
_____
_____

c. **Be aware of how others affect you:** How you feel is affected by the company you keep, whether you are aware of it or not. Studies show that emotions are contagious. We quickly "catch" moods from others — even from strangers who never speak a word. The people you spend a lot of time with have an even greater impact on your mental state.
GROUP DISCUSSION: How can someone else's mood affect you?

A Better Way: Real Talk with Real People

Facilitator, provide a personal response.

_____
_____
_____
_____

d. **Holding grudges:** Who hasn't been hurt by the actions or words of another? Perhaps a parent constantly criticized you while growing up, a colleague sabotaged a project, or your partner had an affair. Maybe you experienced a traumatic experience, such as being physically or emotionally abused by someone close to you.
GROUP DISCUSSION: Why is it so hard to let go of grudges?
Facilitator, provide a personal response.

_____
_____
_____
_____

Those wounds can leave you with lasting feelings of anger and bitterness—even vengeance.

e. **Unforgiving spirit:** If you do not practice forgiveness, you might be the one who pays most dearly. By embracing forgiveness, you can also embrace peace, hope, gratitude, and joy. Consider how not forgiving someone can lead you down the path of physical, emotional, and spiritual chaos.
GROUP DISCUSSION: What happens when a person has an unforgiving spirit? How does that affect a relationship?
Facilitator, provide a personal response.

_____
_____
_____
_____

A Better Way: Real Talk with Real People

If you are unforgiving, you might:

> ➤ Bring anger and bitterness into every relationship and new experience.
> ➤ Become so wrapped up in the wrong, you can't enjoy the present.
> ➤ Lose valuable and enriching connectedness with others.

f. **Comparing yourself to others:** The tendency to compare ourselves to others is as human as any other emotion, but it is a decision that only steals joy from our lives. It is also a habit with numerous shortcomings. **GROUP DISCUSSION:** In what ways do we compare ourselves to other people? How does that affect the way we think of ourselves? Facilitator, provide a personal response.

_____
_____
_____
_____

Facilitator, discuss any or all of the following statements:

Comparisons are always unfair. You typically compare the worst you know of yourself to the best you presume about others.

You are too unique to compare fairly. Your gifts, talents, successes, contributions, and value are entirely unique to you and your purpose in this world. They can never be properly compared to anyone else.

You have nothing to gain, but much to lose – for example, your pride, your dignity, your drive, and your passion.

There is no end to the possible number of comparisons. This negative habit can never be overcome, even by attaining success. There will always be something or someone else on which to focus.

Comparison puts focus on the wrong person. You can control one life: yours. When you always compare yourself to others, you waste precious energy focusing on other people's lives rather than your own.

Comparisons often result in resentment – resentment towards others and even yourself.

Comparisons deprive you of joy: They add no value, meaning, or fulfillment to your life. They only distract from it.

Indeed, the adverse effects of comparisons are wide and far-reaching. Likely, you have experienced (or are experiencing) many of them first-hand in your life as well.

5. **You are lonely vs. being alone:** A lot of people get confused between being alone and experiencing loneliness. Although both are pillars that support the same emotion, there is a distinct difference between the two. Being **alone** is finding a sense of freedom in that isolation, whereas **loneliness** is the isolation that comes with an expectation unmet or having a feeling be unreturned.

Facilitator, discuss any or all of the following statements:

Loneliness is a sense of emotional abandonment.
Being alone is physical and mental freedom.
Loneliness stems from blaming oneself.
Being alone comes from loving oneself.
Loneliness is the feeling of being disconnected.
Being alone is connecting with oneself.
Loneliness is depending on someone else for happiness.
Being alone is finding your own happiness.
Loneliness is longing for something that doesn't exist.
Being alone is enjoying everything that exists in solitude.
Loneliness is rooted in fear.
Being alone is rooted in peace.

A Better Way: Real Talk with Real People

GROUP DISCUSSION: Why do you think people feel lonely when they are alone? What can they do to change that feeling of loneliness? Facilitator, provide a personal response.

_____
_____
_____
_____

Know yourself; be happy!

Facilitator, distribute comment cards, and have each class member write one thing they gained from this class.

A Better Way: Real Talk with Real People
Week 3 – Baggage: Anger

1. Begin class with a discussion from Week 2 – Happy vs. Unhappy. Ask and allow a short question-answer period.

2. **What is Baggage?** Baggage in a relationship is any event, belief, childhood experience, or way of viewing the world that affects how you react to your partner or people in general.

    Let's pretend you are going to take a short trip across town. You will only be gone for about an hour or so, but you begin to worry about what might happen while you're gone. You worry that your car might break down, so you pack up all your tools to repair your car. Then, you begin to worry that someone might break into your home and steal all your valuables, so you pack them up and put them in the car. Then, you worry your house might catch on fire and burn down while you're gone, so you rent a U-Haul and pack up all your furniture and take it with you.

    Of course, that scenario is ridiculous, but that's precisely what we do with the emotional baggage we collect along the way.

Let's now name some of the emotional baggage people carry around. Facilitator, write the following on a whiteboard or easel (if available):

- Worry
- Guilt
- Shame
- Anger
- Bad choices
- Mistakes

Encourage the group to add to the list.

GROUP DISCUSSION: How does emotional baggage affect relationships?

Facilitator, provide a personal response.

_____
_____
_____
_____

3. **That excess baggage called "Anger."**

   a. **Anger:** Anger is a normal emotion to feel, just like happiness or sadness. It can even sometimes motivate us into positive action. However, when anger is not expressed healthily and positively, it can lead to all sorts of problems for ourselves, family members, and anyone else we might be in a relationship with. We all have 'stuff' that has happened to us. Anger can be caused by internal or external events, such as a long, debilitating illness or a sudden traffic jam when you're already running late. Memories of a past event can also trigger feelings of anger. It is those lingering images that we refuse to release that are the most harmful. We use a variety of ways to process our anger.

A Better Way: Real Talk with Real People

GROUP DISCUSSION: Name some ways that we express anger.
Facilitator, provide a personal response.

_____
_____
_____
_____

In some situations, we tend to suppress our anger, particularly if it is an "old" hurt, such as something someone did to us in the past. We hold onto that same anger we felt at the time it happened. Then, we get mad all over again. How many times have we heard or felt that way? Getting mad all over again does not bring closure to the wound. It's like that scab that miraculously appears to shield a wound to give it time to heal. If we leave it alone, the wound will heal.

Conversely, if we continually pick at it, we just keep opening that "old" wound. That's how "old" anger is. We just keep picking at it until it becomes an open sore, never allowed to heal.

GROUP DISCUSSION: What are some of the reasons for past hurts that can still make people angry?
Facilitator, provide a personal response.

_____
_____
_____
_____

One of the biggest obstacles to our personal growth is anger. When we fail to deal with our anger, it can destroy our ability to be happy. It is impossible to be happy if we are constantly in a state of anger. It also compromises any relationships we might have. No one wants to be around a person who is always mad about something.

A Better Way: Real Talk with Real People

It's all in how you look at life. If you get up in the morning, angry about something that happened yesterday, trust me: you will find something to be angry about today. Life then becomes a vicious cycle because of your angry state of mind. Everything that happens just makes you angrier. When the intensity of your anger causes you to make bad decisions—often with adverse consequences—that's an indication that you are not controlling your anger.

GROUP DISCUSSION: What are some of the consequences of a decision made in anger?

Facilitator, provide a personal response.

_____
_____
_____
_____

4. **How do we let go of anger?**
   a. **First, we must determine the cause of the anger.** Often, we are angry at someone else when we need to direct that anger inward. When anger at someone else causes us to make a wrong decision, we will quickly blame that person. However, if we take a hard, truthful look at the point of our anger, we may find that it leads right back to us. Until we get to the root of our anger, we cannot do what needs to be done to let it go.

   GROUP DISCUSSION: Think of someone with whom you're angry. If you could change the situation, what would you change?

   Facilitator, provide a personal response.

   _____
   _____
   _____
   _____

   b. **Second, we must determine if we have learned anything from the past.** We cannot expect different results if we keep doing the same thing. That's the definition of "insanity."

A Better Way: Real Talk with Real People

So, if your response to situations is always angry or cynical, all your future circumstances will have the same result. Your mind is like a bank: it can only withdraw what has been deposited. As such, if all your thoughts are angry, all your resulting actions will also be out of anger. If you have truly looked at the origin of your anger, there should be a lesson for you to learn. That's what life is: a lesson. If we don't learn from our lessons, we will continue to repeat them.

GROUP DISCUSSION: How can you grow from past lessons?

Facilitator, provide a personal response.

_____
_____
_____
_____

c. **What can you do to resolve the anger that still lingers from the past?**
Do you even want to resolve it and get to a place of peace in your spirit? It is a sad reality that some people do not want to change. Are you willing to do what needs to be done to bring a peaceful resolution? When someone you love hurts you, it's very easy to become angry and confused.

If we continue to dwell on those situations, grudges filled with resentment and hostility may take root. If we allow those negative feelings to crowd out our positive ones, we may find ourselves swallowed up in a sea of bitterness. We must be prepared to make some changes in our lives.

GROUP DISCUSSION: What can be done to get past "old" anger?

Facilitator, provide a personal response.

_____
_____
_____
_____

d. **Take control of your thoughts.** Simply put, this means changing the way you think. When you find yourself thinking of past situations or circumstances that made you angry, don't dwell on them. If you continually think about things that make you angry, you add fuel to that anger. Learn to redirect your mind to things that are good and peaceful to your spirit. Think of something funny, instead!
GROUP DISCUSSION: What do people generally do when they think of something that makes them mad?
Facilitator, provide a personal response.

_____
_____
_____
_____

e. **Associate with happy people.** The old saying, *"Misery loves company,"* is true because the only people who want to associate with miserable, angry people are those who are also miserable and angry. You cannot improve your situation if you don't enlarge your territory and seek out new people and new adventures. If you are angry about something, find a true friend who will let you 'vent' (another word for a pity-party).
GROUP DISCUSSION: Why do people hold grudges?
Facilitator, provide a personal response.

_____
_____
_____
_____

f. **Think of your past as a backpack that you've been carrying around all of your life.** The older you are, the heavier your backpack becomes — particularly if you are carrying around old hurts and old anger. You may need to take an inventory of what you're carrying around. You may also need to identify some past hurts that made you angry and prioritize them according to their level of importance.

A Better Way: Real Talk with Real People

You may find you are carrying baggage that is of no importance to your life today. Once you have done that, ask yourself: Is this a memory worth holding onto?

GROUP DISCUSSION: Name some pieces of emotional baggage that weigh people down.

Facilitator, provide a personal response.

_____
_____
_____
_____

Sometimes, people have a lot of anger inside of them due to things that have happened to them in the past: abuse, broken relationships, bereavement, etc. Maybe they feel as if life has treated them badly or unfairly. It's normal to have a lot of anger because of certain situations. Yes, life is sometimes unfair. Yes, there are times when things don't work out the way we want them to or thought they would. However, holding onto past anger because of something that cannot be changed will only damage your life both now and in the future. Yesterday is gone. We cannot get it back. We must do all we can to create a happy life now by releasing those past hurts and past anger. You can choose to stay angry at the world and allow it to destroy your happiness **OR** you can choose to release the anger and begin to heal and start living life to its fullest.

Facilitator, distribute comment cards, and have each class member write one thing they gained from this class.

A Better Way: Real Talk with Real People
Week 4 – Controlling Your Life

1. Begin class with a discussion from Week 3 – Baggage: Anger. Ask and allow a short question-answer period.

Definition of controlling your life: To take control of your life is to take responsibility for yourself and every area of your life. It means being connected with your values and vision while setting meaningful goals for yourself.

PART I

Why do we lose control of our lives?

Have you ever wondered why it is that so many people feel lost in life, not knowing who they are, where they are going, and whether there is any purpose or meaning in their lives? We all have felt that way at one time.
GROUP DISCUSSION: How do we get lost in life?
Facilitator, provide a personal response.

_____
_____
_____
_____

A Better Way: Real Talk with Real People

Let's look at some of the reasons we may find ourselves in this frame of mind.

a. **We have lost the connection with our own hearts and souls.**
   One of the many reasons why people feel lost in life is because they have become disconnected from their own hearts and souls. They pay too much attention to their rational minds and to what everyone else has to say, and now, they can no longer hear the voices of their hearts. Neither can they connect to the wisdom of their souls.
   GROUP DISCUSSION: What can happen when we listen to our heart and not the wisdom of our soul—when something tells us it wasn't right—but we proceeded anyway?
   Facilitator, provide a personal response.

   _____
   _____
   _____
   _____

b. **We live our lives based on what other people believe to be right.**
   Another reason why people feel lost in life is that they live their lives based on what other people believe to be right for them—based on what other people think to be true. They craft their lives based on the thoughts, beliefs, and ideas that were handed down to them from a very young age by their parents, family members, teachers, friends, society, and every single person with whom they interacted. Since they never took the time to question the authenticity of those beliefs and whether they had anything to do with who they truly are, they continued to build, craft, and shape their lives based on what other people believe to be right.
   GROUP DISCUSSION: What happens when a decision you make is based on what someone else said is right for you?

A Better Way: Real Talk with Real People

Facilitator, provide a personal response.

_____
_____
_____
_____

c. **We tend to value the opinions of others more than our own.**
Even though people have a very wise and trusted counselor within themselves—their heart and soul—they don't seem to trust themselves. They constantly seek advice from others, and the opinions of those around them always seem to be more valuable and more important than their own.
GROUP DISCUSSION: Why does someone else's opinion matter more than yours?
Facilitator, provide a personal response.

_____
_____
_____
_____

d. **We have a distorted sense of self.**
People who feel lost in life tend to have a distorted sense of self. They no longer see their true self, their light, and their perfection. They can no longer accept this truth: Who they are is enough! Their vision of reality seems to be darkened and distorted, and all they seem to 'see' is how little, unworthy, and insignificant they are. Nothing they do seems to be good enough.
GROUP DISCUSSION: Why do you think people tend to concentrate more on their negatives than their positives?

A Better Way: Real Talk with Real People

Facilitator, provide a personal response.

_____
_____
_____
_____

e. **We surround ourselves with people who drag us down.**
Spending too much time with the wrong crowd is another reason why so many people feel lost in life. When you surround yourself with people who drag you down—those who are constantly whining, blaming, criticizing, gossiping, and complaining about everything and everyone—you will find your mind, heart, and life poisoned with their fears, doubts, and negativity. Eventually, you will get derailed from your life path, and that will cause you to feel lost.
GROUP DISCUSSION: Name something in which your circle of friends could contribute to a negative situation in your life.
Facilitator, provide a personal response.

_____
_____
_____
_____

f. **We believe every toxic thought that runs through our minds.**
Eckhart Tolle said it so beautifully: *"The mind is a superb instrument if used rightly. Used wrong, however, it becomes very destructive. To put it more accurately: It is not so much that you misuse your mind—you usually don't use it at all. It uses you. All the things that truly matter—beauty, love, creativity, joy, inner peace—arise from beyond the mind..."* When you believe every toxic thought that runs through your mind, and when you insist on building your sense of self and your entire life is based on those thoughts, you can't help but feel lost.
GROUP DISCUSSION: Name some toxic thoughts you have believed about yourself. Why do you think people believe toxic thoughts about themselves?

A Better Way: Real Talk with Real People

Facilitator, provide a personal response.

_____
_____
_____
_____

g. **We are stuck in the past.**
   People are very attached to their past and everything that happened in it. They seemingly cannot find a way to free themselves from it, nor do they want to.
   GROUP DISCUSSION: Why do you think people hold onto negative situations from their past?
   Facilitator, provide a personal response.

_____
_____
_____
_____

PART II

How do you begin to take control of your life?

a. **Change your thinking.** Figure out what taking control of your life means to you. Is it the ability to influence your destiny, regulate your present, and keep your negative behavior in check, or do you simply want more willpower? Taking control of your life requires working through multiple challenges, including your own perceptions and building self-confidence, as well as taking action. Determine what you want more control over, and that will help you focus your energy.
GROUP DISCUSSION: How can you challenge yourself to change your way of thinking?
Facilitator, provide a personal response.

_____
_____
_____
_____

b. **Accept yourself.** The first step to succeeding in anything is knowing and accepting both your strengths and limitations. Show compassion for yourself. Accept not only the good but the bad, too. Always strive to improve the things you don't like or that you struggle with. Understand why you do what you do, then forgive yourself. Self-reflection is healthy and positive. Self-criticism and feeling guilty are unproductive behaviors that do more harm than good.
GROUP DISCUSSION: Name a situation when you were not proud of what you did. Why do you think you did that thing?
Facilitator, provide a personal response.

_____
_____
_____
_____

c. **Consider your values.** You must determine what your values are so that you can get your priorities in order. Think about what and who is important to you.

Have each member of the class list five values from the list provided. Then, have them place them in order from the most important to the least important.

Facilitator, write the list on a whiteboard or easel (if available).

- Dependability
- Loyalty
- Commitment
- Honesty
- Good humor
- Compassion
- Motivation
- Positivity
- Optimism
- Passion
- Respect
- Courage
- Perseverance

GROUP DISCUSSION: Why did you choose those five as the most important?

Facilitator, provide a personal response.

_____
_____
_____
_____

Think about what you are doing right now to support each of your values and how they are affecting your life. It can help to consider what a person whom you respect would think of your values and whether they would influence you to change what they are.

A Better Way: Real Talk with Real People

Think about the person you want to be and what character traits, ways of thinking, behavior patterns, and life you would have as that person.

GROUP DISCUSSION: Name one character trait you would like people to define you by. Why did you choose that trait?

Ask the group how they would describe you (the facilitator) in one word.

Facilitator, provide a personal response.

_____
_____
_____
_____

d. **Cultivate good character traits.** When you improve beneficial character traits and virtues, you will gain more control over your life. This is because having these traits will encourage you to obtain your goals and adopt other qualities you want. Good traits to work on for this purpose are temperance and self-discipline.

Temperance (moderation or self-restraint) is essential because it allows you to maintain perspective, calmness, and self-control. For instance, showing restraint from arrogance by behaving with humility can prevent you from destroying relationships.

Self-discipline is imperative to gaining control of your life because it allows you to put all your intentions into action. Practice self-control daily by making small changes and sticking to them.

GROUP DISCUSSION: How do these traits benefit you? What can you do to improve these traits in yourself?

Facilitator, provide a personal response.

_____
_____
_____
_____

e. **Decide what motivates you.** Many of us have a passion—something that we enjoy and that drives us to succeed. Think about what you would like to do in life if nothing stood in your way. If you don't know, then you will need to write down the activities you like to do that make you feel good. Consider what inspires you, as well as your skills and talents.
GROUP DISCUSSION: Name something you would do, even if you didn't get paid to do it. This is your passion.
Facilitator, provide a personal response.

_____
_____
_____
_____

f. **Create goals.** Find out what you really want out of life this year. Is it a house, a good job, or a healthy relationship? Write down each goal and then come up with ideas that can help you accomplish that goal. Turn each idea into a positive action statement, such as, *"I will save money."* Then, review each of your goals and ideas, choose three of them, and make three action statements for each.
GROUP DISCUSSION: Name something you'd like to accomplish within the next year. What would stop you from achieving that goal?
Facilitator, provide a personal response.

_____
_____
_____
_____

Don't be afraid to modify your goals and ideas as time progresses and you determine what works and what doesn't. The point here is that you take control of your life and the direction in which you are headed.

g. **Get control of your emotions.** Emotions can be wonderful experiences, but expressing them improperly can harm your ability to attain goals as well as damage relationships. You need to learn how to understand, process, and respond to your feelings in a way that is both healthy and helpful to you.
GROUP DISCUSSION: Why do we lose control of our emotions?
Facilitator, provide a personal response.

_____
_____
_____
_____

h. **Release the baggage.** Sometimes, negative thoughts or experiences can be tough to release. You may feel as if they define you or they may be so routine, you may be afraid to be without them. Perhaps it could be as simple as you do not know how to let go. Learning to release past baggage will help you to become more solution-oriented, broaden your vision, and help you take control of your life.
GROUP DISCUSSION: How does carrying emotional baggage affect your life?
Facilitator, provide a personal response.

_____
_____
_____
_____

i. **Make lifestyle changes.** If you are codependent on others for your emotional health or lifestyle, or if you need them to tell you what to do, you are not in control of your life. Learn to solve your problems by spending time alone to think and reflect.
GROUP DISCUSSION: How can you be more independent so that you can better control your life?

A Better Way: Real Talk with Real People

Facilitator, provide a personal response.

_____
_____
_____
_____

j. **Develop positive relationships.** Surround yourself with people who share similar values and goals. You should associate with those who are already where you are trying to get to. Meet new people at places or events that support your values or goals.
GROUP DISCUSSION: How can the people you associate with effect your life?
Facilitator, provide a personal response.

_____
_____
_____
_____

k. **Take action.** You can have all the goals in the world but never get anywhere if you don't take action to achieve them. Do what you must to get what and where you want. Take small steps, but be sure to do something every day that helps you get closer to your goal.
GROUP DISCUSSION: Name one step you can take to accomplish a goal.
Facilitator, provide a personal response.

_____
_____
_____
_____

Facilitator, distribute comment cards, and have each class member write one thing they gained from this class.

A Better Way: Real Talk with Real People
Week 5 – Forgiveness

1. Begin class with a discussion from Week 4 – Controlling Your Life. Ask and allow a short question-answer period.

   Definition of forgiveness: A conscious, deliberate decision to release feelings of resentment or vengeance toward a person or group who has harmed you, regardless of whether they actually deserve your forgiveness.

   GROUP DISCUSSION: Think of a situation when you forgave someone. How did that make you feel? Now, think of a situation when someone forgave you. How did that make you feel?
   Facilitator, provide a personal response.

   _____
   _____
   _____
   _____

Forgiveness makes it clear that when you forgive, you do not gloss over or deny the seriousness of an offense against you. Forgiveness does not mean forgetting. Nor does it mean condoning or excusing offenses. Although forgiveness can help repair a damaged relationship, it doesn't obligate you to reconcile with the person who harmed you or release them from legal accountability.

Instead, forgiveness brings the forgiver peace of mind and frees them from corrosive anger. Anger only hurts the host. Forgiving another involves releasing deeply-held negative feelings. In that way, you are empowered to recognize the pain you suffered without letting that pain define you, which enables you to heal and move on with your life.

GROUP DISCUSSION: What does forgiveness mean to you?

Facilitator, provide a personal definition.

_____

_____

_____

_____

GROUP DISCUSSION:

1. **What forgiveness doesn't mean:**

    ➢ Forgiveness doesn't mean you are pardoning or excusing the other person's actions.
    ➢ Forgiveness doesn't mean you need to tell the person that he or she is forgiven.
    ➢ Forgiveness doesn't mean you shouldn't have any more feelings about the situation.
    ➢ Forgiveness doesn't mean there is nothing further to work out in the relationship or that everything is okay now.
    ➢ Forgiveness doesn't mean you should forget the incident ever happened.
    ➢ Forgiveness doesn't mean you must continue to include the person in your life.
    ➢ Forgiveness isn't something you do for the other person.

A Better Way: Real Talk with Real People

GROUP DISCUSSION: What do you think are some of the benefits of forgiving someone?
Facilitator, provide a personal response.

_____
_____
_____
_____

Letting go of grudges and bitterness makes way for compassion, kindness, and peace. Forgiveness can lead to:

- Healthier relationships
- Greater spiritual and psychological well-being
- Less stress and hostility
- Lower blood pressure
- Fewer symptoms of depression, anxiety, and chronic pain
- Lower risk of alcohol and substance abuse

GROUP DISCUSSION: Why do you think it's so easy to hold a grudge?
Facilitator, provide a personal response.

_____
_____
_____
_____

When you're hurt by someone you love and trust, you may become angry, sad, or confused. If you dwell on hurtful events or situations, grudges filled with resentment, vengeance, and hostility may take root. If you allow negative feelings to crowd out positive ones, you may find yourself swallowed up by your own bitterness or sense of injustice.

2. **What are the effects of holding a grudge?**
   GROUP DISCUSSION: Why do people stay angry?
   Facilitator, provide a personal response.

   _____
   _____
   _____
   _____

   If you're unforgiving, you may pay the price repeatedly by bringing anger and bitterness into every relationship and new experience. Your life may become so wrapped up in the wrong that you can't enjoy the present. You may become depressed or anxious. You may feel that your life lacks meaning or purpose, or that you're at odds with your spiritual beliefs. You may also lose valuable and enriching connectedness with others.

3. **How do you reach a state of forgiveness?**
   GROUP DISCUSSION: What did you learn from that hurtful situation? If you cannot think of anything, think of a lesson that can be learned.
   Facilitator, provide a personal response.

   _____
   _____
   _____
   _____

   Forgiveness is a commitment to a process of change. A way to begin is by recognizing the value of forgiveness and its importance in your life at any given moment. Then, reflect on the facts of the situation, how you've reacted, and how the combination of the two has affected your life, health, and well-being. When you're ready, actively choose to forgive the person who offended you. Move away from your role as victim and release the control and power the offending person and situation have had in your life. As you release grudges, you will no longer define your life by how you've been hurt. You may even find compassion and understanding.

4. **What happens if you can't forgive someone?**
   GROUP DISCUSSION: How can you retrain your thoughts to be more positive about the situation?
   Facilitator, provide a personal response.

   _____
   _____
   _____
   _____

Admittedly, forgiveness can be challenging. It may be particularly difficult to forgive someone who doesn't admit their wrongs or doesn't speak of their sorrow. If you find yourself stuck, it may help to write in a journal, pray, or use guided meditation. You may want to talk with a person you've found to be wise and compassionate, such as a spiritual leader, mental health provider, or an unbiased family member or friend. You may also want to reflect on times you've hurt others and on those who have forgiven you. Keep in mind that forgiveness has the potential to increase your sense of integrity, peace, and overall well-being.

GROUP DISCUSSION QUESTIONS:

1. **Does forgiveness guarantee reconciliation?**
   If the hurtful event involved someone whose relationship you otherwise value, forgiveness may lead to reconciliation. This isn't always the case, however. Reconciliation may be impossible if the offender has died or is unwilling to communicate with you. In other cases, reconciliation may not be appropriate, especially if you were attacked or assaulted. Even in those cases, forgiveness is still possible—even if reconciliation is not.

2. **What if you have to interact with the person who hurt you, but you don't want to?**
   If you have not reached a state of forgiveness, being near the person who hurt you may be tense and stressful. To best handle those situations, remember that you have a choice of whether or not to attend specific functions and gatherings. Respect yourself and do what seems best.

If you choose to attend, don't be surprised by a certain amount of awkwardness and perhaps even more intense feelings.

3. **What if the person you are forgiving doesn't change?**
   Getting another person to change their actions, behaviors, or words isn't the point of forgiveness. Think more about how forgiveness can change your life by bringing you more peace, happiness, and emotional and spiritual healing. Forgiveness takes away the power the other person continues to wield in your life.

4. **What if you are the one who needs forgiving?**
   Consider admitting the wrong you've done to those you've harmed. Speak of your sincere sorrow or regret while specifically asking for forgiveness—without making excuses. Remember, however, that you cannot force someone to forgive you. Others need to move to a state of forgiveness in their own time. Simply acknowledge your faults and admit your mistakes. Then, commit to treating others with compassion, empathy, and respect.

Facilitator, distribute comment cards, and have each class member write one thing they gained from this class.

A Better Way: Real Talk with Real People
Week 6 – Toxic Relationships

1. Begin class with a discussion from Week 5 – Forgiveness. Ask and allow a short question-answer period.

2. **Toxic relationships:** We have all had toxic people dust us with their poison. Sometimes, it's more like a drenching. Difficult people are drawn to the reasonable ones, and all of us have likely had (or have) at least one person in our lives who have us bending around ourselves like barbed wire in endless attempts to please them — only to never really get there.
   GROUP DISCUSSION: How would you describe a toxic relationship? Why was it toxic?
   Facilitator, provide a personal response.

   _____
   _____
   _____

A Better Way: Real Talk with Real People

GROUP DISCUSSION: *Types of toxic people.*

a. **People who spread negativity.** How do you think people spread negativity (i.e., spreading gossip)?
b. **People who waste your time.** How do you waste time (i.e., spending time on meaningless activities)?
c. **People who are jealous.** Why do you think people are jealous (i.e., low self-esteem)?
d. **People who play the victim.** Name something people who play the victim would say (i.e., "It's not my fault").

Facilitator, provide a personal response.

_____
_____
_____
_____

3. **How to Identify Toxic People**

   Toxic people are manipulative. It's all about them. They use other people to accomplish whatever their goal happens to be. They typically have no boundaries in their pursuit of what they want and will totally disregard who gets hurt along the way. They will crowd your space — physically, mentally, emotionally, or whatever — without concern or feeling bad about it.
   GROUP DISCUSSION: How do people use or manipulate someone else to get what they want?
   Facilitator, provide a personal response.

_____
_____
_____
_____

A Better Way: Real Talk with Real People

Toxic people are judgmental. Keep your eyes and ears open for criticism—about you, what you've done, and what you didn't do. They tend to be overly critical and will justify what they say because they believe it to be true. It's never about them, and they will lie if it serves them.

GROUP DISCUSSION: Why do you think some people constantly judge or criticize others?

Facilitator, provide a personal response.

_____
_____
_____
_____

Toxic people take no responsibility for their own feelings. Rather, their feelings are projected onto you. They vehemently defend their perspective and take no responsibility for almost anything they do.

GROUP DISCUSSION: Why do you think it's so difficult for some people to take responsibility for themselves and always blame others?

Facilitator, provide a personal response.

_____
_____
_____
_____

Toxic people do not apologize. They don't see any reason to because things are always someone else's fault. They either see themselves as a victim or think of themselves as perfect. Either way, this type of toxic person can prove difficult to cultivate any kind of meaningful relationship with.

GROUP DISCUSSION: What happens to a relationship where one person never feels they should have to apologize for anything?

A Better Way: Real Talk with Real People

Facilitator, provide a personal response.

_____
_____
_____
_____

Toxic people are inconsistent. It's hard to know who you're with at any given time because they are often not the same person. They may change their attitude and behavior, depending on what they want to happen. We all know people who are fine today, but when you speak to them on another day, they have completely changed their attitude.

GROUP DISCUSSION: How do you deal with a person who changes from day to day?

Facilitator, provide a personal response.

_____
_____
_____
_____

Toxic people make you prove yourself to them. Toxic people make you choose them over someone else or something they want over something you want, even to the point of requiring you to cut off other relationships just to satisfy them.

GROUP DISCUSSION: Think of a controlling person and a situation when they want someone to choose their way, even if it's not the best way. How do you think that situation turns out?

Facilitator, provide a personal response.

_____
_____
_____
_____

A Better Way: Real Talk with Real People

Do any of the following sound familiar?

> - You've been friends for years. She's always been prickly, but now you're noticing her zingers are louder than ever and aimed directly at you.
> - Your coworker is a show-off who's always dismissed your suggestions and ideas. Now, he's actively disparaging you to anyone who will listen.
> - Your partner says mean things to you, and when you object, he either says, "You're too sensitive," or stonewalls and refuses to talk.
> - Your parent has amped up the volume on putting you down, no matter what.

GROUP DISCUSSION: How should you react to those kinds of people?

Facilitator, provide a personal response.

_____
_____
_____
_____

4. How to Deal with Toxic People

Set and maintain boundaries. Boundaries are important in general, but they become especially important when you're dealing with toxic people. They often take advantage of those with poorly-defined boundaries and low self-assertiveness. First, you must identify your boundaries. They will consist of what you will and will not accept from someone else (i.e., attitude, behavior, etc.).

GROUP DISCUSSION: What is your definition of personal boundaries regarding how people treat you?

A Better Way: Real Talk with Real People

Facilitator, provide a personal response.

_____
_____
_____
_____

Listen to your gut. It's easy for some people to make excuses for a toxic person. You may know deep down that the person is bad for you or is taking advantage of you. Avoid rationalizing those gut instincts or explaining the toxic person's behavior away. When your gut tells you something is not right with someone, listen to it and stop making excuses for their bad behavior.

GROUP DISCUSSION: What are some of the excuses we use to justify someone's bad behavior?

Facilitator, provide a personal response.

_____
_____
_____
_____

Take responsibility for what you're doing. Try to make a sober assessment of the kind of relationship you're in and the effect it is having on you. Many people who continue being friends with toxic people have a "people pleaser" personality. They want to be liked and made to feel as if they're supporting others at all costs. Ask yourself, *"Why am I still associating with this person?"*

GROUP DISCUSSION: Why do people maintain relationships with those they know aren't good for them?

Facilitator, provide a personal response.

_____
_____
_____
_____

A Better Way: Real Talk with Real People

Walk away. At the end of the day, you may need to end your relationship with the person if it is toxic. Cutting people out of your life can be a painful exercise, but in the case of toxic people, short-term pain can be healthier than long-term pain.

Facilitator, distribute comment cards, and have each class member write one thing they gained from this class.

A Better Way: Real Talk with Real People
Week 7 – Guilt

How often have you convicted yourself for a crime you either didn't commit or couldn't have changed the outcome? Guilt is a normal emotional signal we learn early in our childhood development. Its purpose is to warn us when we've done something wrong and to help us see how our behavior impacts not only ourselves but also those around us. Guilt should lead us to examine our decisions so that we don't continue to make the same mistakes. We must learn how to deal with our guilty feelings by either accepting them when they are important or letting them go when they are not. To do that, we must recognize what type of guilt we are dealing with.

GROUP DISCUSSION: Why do we feel guilty?
Facilitator, provide a personal response.

_____
_____
_____
_____

A Better Way: Real Talk with Real People

1. **Types of Guilt**

    a. **Healthy guilt** is our conscience, telling us that we have done something against our morals and beliefs. It's that little voice that says, "You know you shouldn't have been there in the first place" or "Why did you do that?" This type of guilt should convict you to take appropriate actions to rectify the situation. It requires us to admit we may have made a bad decision, take responsibility, and live with the consequences.

    Examples of Healthy Guilt:

    ➤ Not taking care of our responsibilities.
    ➤ Procrastinating about an important task or project that we should have already completed.
    ➤ Hurting our friends or loved ones.
    ➤ Telling a "white lie" to back out of a commitment you made.

    GROUP DISCUSSION: What lessons can we learn from healthy guilt?
    Facilitator, provide a personal response.

    _____
    _____
    _____
    _____

    b. **Unhealthy guilt** happens when you feel everything is your fault—even when you didn't do anything wrong. Sometimes, things are totally beyond your control, yet, somehow, you feel responsible. Our children are a perfect example of unhealthy guilt. Of course, you want everything to be perfect in their lives, but when they become adults, we cannot feel responsible for the decisions they make. We equate our worthiness by the failures of others.

Examples of Unhealthy Guilt:
- ➤ One can feel as though they have done something wrong when their reality does not show this to be the case.
- ➤ When another person looks upset or down, one can feel that it is their fault.
- ➤ There could be a situation where one is given something, but instead of feeling worthy, they feel unworthy.
- ➤ One might have achieved a specific goal or overcome a particular challenge and, instead of feeling good about it, they end up feeling uncomfortable and unworthy.

GROUP DISCUSSION: Why do we feel bad about something that wasn't even our fault?
Facilitator, provide a personal response.

_____
_____
_____
_____

c. **False guilt** occurs with people who see themselves as victims. People who have experienced abuse or violent crimes sometimes feel it was their fault and begin to accept the blame. This false guilt is unhealthy and can lead to other serious consequences. People who have self-destructive behavior patterns often deal with issues of false guilt. They perpetuate the victim syndrome because they are overcome with the fear of making wrong decisions, so they allow someone to make decisions for them. They tend to rely on someone else's beliefs and comments.

Examples of False Guilt:
- ➤ You feel stuck or trapped, especially if you think there are no alternatives open to you.
- ➤ You're protecting someone else's feelings.
- ➤ You've apologized and made amends, yet you *STILL* feel guilty.

A Better Way: Real Talk with Real People

GROUP DISCUSSION: Name a situation when you felt stuck or when you were protecting someone else's feelings at your expense. How do you think that way of thinking affects a relationship?
Facilitator, provide a personal response.

_____
_____
_____
_____

d. Toxic guilt seeps into all areas of an individual's life and destroys their health and happiness. It causes stress, which compromises the immune system and increases vulnerability to illness. Some forms of guilt can be a positive force by steering people to do the right thing, but there is a big difference between good and bad guilt. The former teaches you to consider the needs of others and helps you to choose right from wrong; the latter stems from insecurity, hyper-sensitivity to how others perceive you, and a desperate need to be liked. People with toxic guilt are continually striving to be good enough, bent on pleasing those around them, and enslaved by unreasonably high expectations of themselves.

Examples of Toxic Guilt:
- Is pleasing others the driving force in your life?
- Does the need to see yourself as "good" motivate you to take on people or projects when you'd really rather not?
- Do you feel you're never quite good enough?
- Would you like to change something about your life—such as moving to another place or ending an unhealthy relationship—but won't because you'd feel too guilty?
- Do you habitually give more than you receive?

GROUP DISCUSSION: Why do you think we constantly sacrifice ourselves for someone else and then feel we're always giving and never receiving as much as we give?

A Better Way: Real Talk with Real People

Facilitator, provide a personal response.

_____
_____
_____
_____

2. **How people use your guilt to their advantage.**

   a. **People will make requests of you and then make you think they will suffer if you don't do what they ask.** You will end up accepting responsibility for someone else's problems or misfortunes because it will bother you to see them suffer. Ultimately, you will find yourself doing something that someone else wants you to do that makes them happy, but you unhappy. They will call on your guilt or shame to do what they want, even if it violates your rights. That's called victimization.
   GROUP DISCUSSION: What happens when we compromise what we want to make another person happy?
   Facilitator, provide a personal response.

   _____
   _____
   _____
   _____

   b. **People will reinforce your negative, irrational thinking by forcing you to have a sense of blame for past, present, and any future actions.** Often, these actions are beyond your control, yet, if you are not careful, people will force total responsibility for their misfortune. It's incredible how people who don't take responsibility for their own actions will be quick to point out to someone else how it's "their fault" that something terrible happened. If we are truthful with ourselves, we will see how our own actions result in the consequences of our behavior.

A Better Way: Real Talk with Real People

GROUP DISCUSSION: We can be made to feel that someone else's actions are our fault for something we may or may not have done in the past. Why do you think we feel guilty?
Facilitator, provide a personal response.

_____
_____
_____
_____

c. **People will verbally assault you by creating an environment where you feel you are at fault, even when there has been no action on your part.** This will force you into thinking you have to do whatever you can to alleviate the situation, thus causing you to make unhealthy decisions, which further guarantees your sense of shame and guilt. Now, you are in a vicious cycle of blame and guilt, further reinforcing your negative self-perceptions.
GROUP DISCUSSION: We sometimes compromise ourselves for someone else and then make an unhealthy decision. What are some of the possible consequences of that decision?
Facilitator, provide a personal response.

_____
_____
_____
_____

d. **People will threaten negative consequences to manipulate your guilt and shame.** This will cause you to make decisions to accommodate the manipulator at your expense. After a while, you will be unable to make any decisions, lest it is the wrong one. You begin a pattern of denying yourself, believing it's actually better to serve others than yourself.
GROUP DISCUSSION: Think of a situation when someone might feel it was better just to do what someone asked them to do because of implied consequences. How do you think that made them feel?

Facilitator, provide a personal response.

_____
_____
_____
_____

3. **How do you heal from past guilt?**

   Healing from past guilt requires forgiveness and letting go of what used to be so that you can now enjoy the fullness of life. How do we move past the guilt? We must learn how to manage it.

   a. **Recognize and identify your feelings of guilt.** You must deal with the reason for your guilt. Once you determine why you're feeling guilty, you can begin to move forward to release yourself from those feelings. It may require you to return to a painful part of your past and deal with some raw emotions. It is only when you can identify the cause of your guilty feelings that you can create harmony within yourself. Is your guilt healthy, unhealthy, or false?
   GROUP DISCUSSION: What are some things you may feel guilty about? Why do you still feel guilty?
   Facilitator, provide a personal response.

   _____
   _____
   _____
   _____

   b. **Acknowledge your role in the wrongdoing to yourself or others.** As mature adults, we must accept a certain amount of responsibility for some situations. Have you examined yourself to see what your role was? By not acknowledging that, you perpetuate the guilty feelings you may be having. Accepting responsibility for your actions and your life is one of the most important aspects of personal development.

A Better Way: Real Talk with Real People

GROUP DISCUSSION: Think of a situation when you might feel guilty. What could have been done differently?
Facilitator, provide a personal response.

_____
_____
_____
_____

c. **Are you getting any positive experiences from feeling guilty? Guilt demonstrates that you have a conscience.** Psychologists, such as Suffolk University professor Jane Bybee, say, *"Guilt is useful because it gets people to regret the wrong they do and correct it. They feel a sense of remorse over it. They wish that they could undo it. They feel, they ruminate, or they think deeply over it."*
GROUP DISCUSSION: How can guilt be used to create a better relationship?
Facilitator, provide a personal response.

_____
_____
_____
_____

d. **Learn from the situation, so you don't repeat the same mistakes.** Guilt's purpose isn't to make you feel bad just for the sake of it. The feeling of guilt is trying to get your attention so that you can learn something from the experience. If you learn from your behavior, you will be less likely to do it again in the future. While we sometimes already know the lesson that guilt is trying to teach us, it will return time and time again until we've actually learned the lesson fully.
GROUP DISCUSSION: Think of a situation that can make you feel guilty because of a mistake you made. What behavior can be changed, so it doesn't happen again?

A Better Way: Real Talk with Real People

Facilitator, provide a personal response.

_____
_____
_____
_____

    e. **Let go of the past and move on.** Letting go of your past means accepting that there's nothing you can do to change the past. You did the best you could. When you're facing your past decisions or actions, know that you were as good, loving, and effective as you could have been. If you were to go back, you couldn't do anything differently because that's who you were; that's what you knew then. It is done. Let go of your past. Accept and acknowledge the inappropriate behavior, make your amends, and move on.
GROUP DISCUSSION: Think of a past situation that can still make you feel guilty. What can be done to change that thinking to move past that feeling of guilt?
Facilitator, provide a personal response.

_____
_____
_____
_____

We all make mistakes. Many of us go down a path in our lives that can make us feel guilty later after realizing our mistakes. The key, however, is to realize the error and accept that you're only human. Don't engage in days, weeks, or months of self-blame or battering your self-esteem because you "should've known," "should've acted differently," or "should've been an ideal person." You're not, and neither am I. That's just life!

Facilitator, distribute comment cards, and have each class member write one thing they gained from this class.

A Better Way: Real Talk with Real People

Week 8 – Controlling Your Thoughts

1. Begin class with a discussion from Week 7 – Guilt. Ask and allow a short question-answer period.

Controlling Your Thoughts

Your mind is the most powerful tool you have for the creation of good in your life, but if not used correctly, it can also be the most destructive force in your life. Your mind—more specifically, your thoughts—affect your perception and, therefore, your interpretation of reality.

There's a statistic that states the average person thinks around **70,000 thoughts a day.** That's a lot, especially if they are unproductive, self-abusive, and just a general waste of energy. You can let your thoughts run amok, but why would you? It is your mind. They are your thoughts. Isn't it time to take your power back? Isn't it time to take control?

A Better Way: Real Talk with Real People

Choose to be the person who is actively and consciously thinking your thoughts. Become the master of your mind. When you change your thoughts, you will change your feelings as well, and you will also eliminate the triggers that set off those feelings. Both outcomes provide you with a greater level of peace of mind.

> **GROUP DISCUSSION:** Do you listen to your thoughts? What are your thoughts saying to you right now?
> Facilitator, provide a personal response.

_____
_____
_____
_____

2. **Who is thinking your thoughts?**

> Before you can become the master of your mind, you must recognize that you are currently at the mercy of several unwanted "squatters" living in your mind, and they are in charge of your thoughts. If you want to be the boss of them, you must know who they are and what their motivation is. Only then can you take charge and evict them.
> GROUP DISCUSSION: What is a squatter? How do you think squatter thoughts affect you?
> Facilitator, give a personal response.

_____
_____
_____
_____

A Better Way: Real Talk with Real People

There are four "squatters" in your head that create the most unhealthy and unproductive thoughts:

a. **The Inner Critic**
   This squatter is motivated by pain, low self-esteem, lack of self-acceptance, and lack of self-love. This is your constant abuser and is often a conglomeration of:
   - Other people's words—many times, your parents.
   - Thoughts you have created based on your own or others' expectations.
   - Comparing yourself to other people, including those in the media.
   - The things you told yourself as a result of painful experiences, such as betrayal and rejection.

GROUP DISCUSSION: Think of a thought that is based on someone else's words. How can that affect your opinion of self?
Facilitator, provide a personal response.

_____
_____
_____
_____

b. **The Worrier**
   This squatter lives in the future—in the world of "what ifs." It is motivated by fear, which is often irrational and without a basis. Occasionally, this squatter's motivation is fear of something that happened in the past happening again. We worry about:
   - Money, bills, debt
   - Careers, jobs, employment/unemployment
   - Children, parents, siblings, friends
   - Making wrong decisions
   - Being happy, being accepted, being alone.

A Better Way: Real Talk with Real People

GROUP DISCUSSION: Name something people worry about. How can they change their thoughts?

Facilitator, provide a personal response.

_____
_____
_____
_____

c. **The Reactor or Troublemaker**

This squatter is the one that triggers anger, frustration, and pain. These triggers stem from unhealed wounds of the past. Any experience that is even closely related to a past wound will set it off, often by words, feelings, sounds, or even smells. Lacking any sense of real motivation, it has poor impulse control and is run by past programming that no longer serves a purpose — if it ever did.

GROUP DISCUSSION: Name a trigger. What do you think makes this a trigger (i.e., a past experience, an old hurt)?

Facilitator, provide a personal response.

_____
_____
_____
_____

d. **The Sleep Depriver**

This can be a combination of any number of different squatters, including the Inner Planner, the Rehasher, and the Contemplator, along with the Inner Critic and the Worrier. Its motivation can be:

> ➢ A reaction to silence, which it fights against.
> ➢ Taking care of the business you neglected during the day.
> ➢ Self-doubt, low self-esteem, insecurity, and generalized anxiety.

A Better Way: Real Talk with Real People

GROUP DISCUSSION: What do you think about when you lay down to sleep? How are those thoughts affecting your mental state? Facilitator, provide a personal response.

_____
_____
_____
_____

3. How can you control these squatters?

How to Master Your Mind:

You are the thinker and the observer of your thoughts. You must pay attention to your thoughts so you can identify "who" is running the show. This will determine which technique you will want to use. Begin each day with the intention of paying attention to your thoughts and catching yourself when you are thinking undesirable thoughts.

There are two ways to control your thoughts:

1. **Technique A** – Interrupt and replace them. (This option is a means of reprogramming your subconscious mind. Eventually, the replaced thoughts will become the "go-to" thoughts in applicable situations.)
2. **Technique B** – Eliminate them altogether. (This option is simply known as peace of mind).

For the Inner Critic

When you catch yourself thinking something negative about yourself (i.e., calling yourself names, disrespecting yourself, or berating yourself), interrupt it. You can yell (in your mind), *"Stop! No!"* or *"Enough! I'm in control now!"* Then, replace whatever negative thought you were having with an opposite thought or an affirmation that begins with **"I am..."**

A Better Way: Real Talk with Real People

You can also have a dialogue with yourself to discredit the 'voice' that created the thought—if you know whose voice it is. Remind yourself, *"Just because so-and-so said I was a loser doesn't make it true. It was their opinion, not a statement of fact. Maybe they were joking, and I took it seriously because I'm insecure."*

If you recognize you have recurring self-critical thoughts, you can write out or pre-plan your counter-thoughts or affirmations so you can be ready. This is the first squatter you should evict—forcefully, if necessary—because it can activate and become a trigger for all of your other squatters. Eliminate your worst critic, and you will also diminish the presence of the other three squatters. Replace it with your new best friend who supports, encourages, and enhances your life. This is a presence you want in your mind.

> **GROUP DISCUSSION:** Name some recurring negative thoughts people tend to have about themselves. From where do those thoughts usually come?
> Facilitator, provide a personal response.

_____
_____
_____
_____

For the Worrier

Prolonged anxiety is mentally, emotionally, and physically unhealthy. It can have long-term health implications. You should be able to recognize a "worry thought" immediately by how you feel. When a worrying thought comes to your mind, acknowledge it for what it is: a thought—nothing more, nothing less. Before you can deal with a situation, you must recognize that it exists.

You should immediately replace your thoughts of worry with thoughts of gratitude for the outcome you desire. If you believe in a higher power, this is the time to engage with it. Instead of worrying about the possibility of something bad happening, say a prayer of gratitude, such as:

A Better Way: Real Talk with Real People

"Thank you, Lord, for watching over and protecting me. I ask that you continue to bless and keep me from all hurt, harm, and danger. Thank You in advance for working this out. Amen."

> **GROUP DISCUSSION:** Think of something that people constantly worry about. What action can be taken to change the situation? Facilitator, provide a personal response.
>
> _____
> _____
> _____
> _____

For the Troublemaker, Reactor, or Over-Reactor

Permanently eliminating this squatter will take a bit more attention and reflection after the fact to identify and heal the causes of the triggers. The Reactor's thoughts or feelings activate the fight or flight response, just like with the Worrier. Have you heard the recommendation to count to ten when you get angry? Well, you can make those ten seconds much more productive if you are breathing consciously during that time.

One of the troubles this squatter causes is that it adds to the Sleep Depriver's issues. By evicting, or at least controlling the Reactor, you will decrease reactionary behavior, which will reduce the need for rehashing and ruminating that may keep you from falling asleep. Master your mind and stop the Reactor from bringing stress to you and your relationships!

> **GROUP DISCUSSION:** Think of a situation that causes people to overreact. If they were more in control of their thoughts, how do you think they would have handled the situation differently?

A Better Way: Real Talk with Real People

Facilitator, provide a personal response.

_____
_____
_____
_____

For the Sleep Depriver
(Comprised of the Inner Planner, the Rehasher, and the Ruminator (deep-thinker), along with the Inner Critic and the Worrier.)

Many people are plagued with a widespread problem: not being able to turn their mind at bedtime. This inability prevents you from falling asleep and, thus, getting a restful and restorative night's sleep. You think about the day you've just completed and what you have on your schedule for tomorrow. Sometimes, your mind will reach way back and think of something that has long since passed. This happens to everyone at one time or another. Once we get too old for a bedtime story, it's not always clear what to do.

Some suggestions on how to master your mind and evict the Sleep Depriver and its cronies include:

➢ Think of something else besides what's worrying you. Perhaps think of what your dream house would look like. Think of the rooms and how you would decorate each. Think of a dream destination. Envision that space in vivid detail.
➢ Sometimes, you have to trick your mind into falling asleep. So, instead of worrying about not being able to go to sleep, become comfortable with the idea of staying awake. If you can become comfortable with that idea, the anxiety and frustration diminish, and you become more relaxed.
➢ Find a peaceful phrase of scripture on which to concentrate. Repeat it over and over until your mind and body are relaxed. With this technique, you are still thinking, but the wheels are no longer spinning out of control. Try repeating short phrases such as, *"I am in control of my mind"* or *"I choose peace and quiet."*

A Better Way: Real Talk with Real People

GROUP DISCUSSION: What thoughts do you find yourself having when trying to go to sleep? What can you do to replace those thoughts so that you can rest?

Facilitator, provide a personal response.

_____
_____
_____
_____

Becoming the Master of Your Mind

Your mind is a tool, and, like any other tool, it can be used for constructive purposes—or destructive purposes. You can allow your mind to be occupied with unwanted, undesirable, and destructive tenants, or you can choose desirable tenants like peace, gratitude, compassion, love, and joy.

Your mind can become your best friend, biggest supporter, and one you can count on to be there and encourage you. The choice is yours!

Facilitator, distribute comment cards, and have each class member write one thing they gained from this class.

A Better Way: Real Talk with Real People
Week 9 – Disappointment

1. Begin class with a discussion from Week 8 – Controlling Your Thoughts. Ask and allow a short question-answer period.

Unfortunately, disappointment is an inevitable emotion that can't be avoided. At some point in our lives, we are either going to be disappointed by someone, or we will be the one to disappoint another who depended on us. When our expectations exceed reality, disappointment is going to occur.

While it's normal to feel disappointment, it is imperative that we learn from the experience and overcome the situation in order to avoid the adverse side effects of not being able to get over it. We must learn how to process the disappointment and the attached emotions in order to maintain a balanced sense of well-being.

A Better Way: Real Talk with Real People

Disappointment is processed in different ways. When some people hit that wall, they shut down. They will sulk and mope, sometimes even moving into a space that looks victim-like. It will become a pity-party of one. Others will get angry and defensive, which can feel like punishment to an already hurting person. Their shame has piled up, and they cannot see straight, much less actually feel meaningful empathy.

> GROUP DISCUSSION: Think of a situation when you disappointed someone. Why do you think people disappoint those they care about?
> Facilitator, provide a personal response.

_____
_____
_____
_____

2. **Why do we get disappointed?**

    Should we lower our expectations?
    Of course, we shouldn't lower our expectations! Many of us start to change the way we think, from being an optimist to being a pessimist, in order to circumvent disappointment. This is a colossal mistake because it's not a solution; it's just an avoidance technique. We must be realistic in our expectations. Are we expecting more than what can be delivered? Adequately dealing with disappointment is a combination of learning to have a positive way of thinking while having a backup plan in the event your expectations don't come full circle.
    GROUP DISCUSSION: Think of a situation that disappointed you because someone didn't live up to your expectations. What is the best way to deal with this kind of disappointment?
    Facilitator, provide a personal response.

_____
_____
_____
_____

A Better Way: Real Talk with Real People

Disappointment and depression.

In cases of continued disappointment, the final step may be depression. Some people are better psychologically equipped to deal with disappointment, while others may be overcome with despair and depression. Being able to deal with disappointment is a particularly important step to prevent depression and in combating false beliefs about yourself, such as, *"There is no hope for me"* or *"Nothing ever works out for me."*

GROUP DISCUSSION: Think of situations in life when you felt a sense of hopelessness (i.e., nothing ever goes right). How did you overcome that state of mind?

Facilitator, provide a personal response.

_____
_____
_____
_____

Overconfidence.

Many people often become disappointed as a result of being overconfident. After all, you expect a lot from yourself, which is why you became disappointed when you didn't perform to your own expectations. If you recognize this person, then understand the champions in life are those who are balanced in life. Such people realize they might not always end up in the Winner's Circle, but they have the ability to manage the inevitable losses.

GROUP DISCUSSION: Think of a time when you were disappointed in yourself. What could you have done differently to achieve the results you wanted?

Facilitator, provide a personal response.

_____
_____
_____
_____

A Better Way: Real Talk with Real People

No backup plan.

Many people go through life with only one plan. If that plan doesn't work out, they have nothing on which to fall back. Have a backup plan in mind in case things don't go according to plan. This will not only make you more secure, but it will also keep you from becoming disappointed should something unexpected happen, which is a very real possibility.

GROUP DISCUSSION: What is the purpose of a backup plan? What lesson can be learned if you don't have such a plan in place?

Facilitator, provide a personal response.

_____
_____
_____
_____

Having false ideas about failure.

One of the leading causes of disappointment is a false idea about what failure is. Failure is only feedback telling you that you should change your way, be more flexible, or try harder. Everyone fails at something at some point in their lives. It may be a failing grade at school, a failure to get a promotion on the job, or failing at love. Disappointment due to failure is unavoidable. Although you wish to experience only successes and no failures, you can't have one without the other. Failure—like success—is a fact of life. It is always lurking just around the corner, and you have no choice but to learn to deal with it if you are to be successful.

GROUP DISCUSSION: How do you define failure? How can failure affect someone?

Facilitator, provide a personal response.

_____
_____
_____
_____

A Better Way: Real Talk with Real People

3. **How do you overcome disappointment and move on?**

Do a reality check. Ask, *"Is it really that bad?"*
After feeling the first blows of disappointment, step back and assess. It can seem like the biggest, most horrible thing that could possibly happen—but we tend to dramatize. *"Feelings are real and are important to recognize, but thoughts are not always the truth,"* says Psychotherapist Sarah Mandel, R.N., L.C.S.W. When the initial upset is over, she recommends *"...looking objectively at your problems to help separate fact from fiction and reduce negative self-talk."*

GROUP DISCUSSION: Think of a situation that you initially thought was worse than what it actually was. How much was fact and how much was what you thought?

Facilitator, provide a personal response.

_____
_____
_____
_____

Don't stew in negativity.
If we're not careful, we'll adopt limiting beliefs such as *"Things never work out"* or *"This always seems to happen to me."* Wallowing in disappointment brought on by a negative mindset keeps people stuck. Everyone gets disappointed at some point in life. We all have pity-parties. The key to getting over this is to know when to stop stewing in the disappointment. The longer you stew, the more likely you will allow yourself to become discouraged, which is even more challenging to overcome. Turn the emotional tables on disappointment by looking for ways to grow from it.

GROUP DISCUSSION: Think of a disappointing situation that caused you to become negative. How can we grow and become better instead of bitter after being disappointed?

A Better Way: Real Talk with Real People

Facilitator, provide a personal response.

_____
_____
_____
_____

Try not to take other people's reactions and opinions to heart.
Differing points of view are not, in themselves, insults. Everybody has their own opinion. We can sometimes feel disappointed if someone disagrees with us. We think it implies we've done something wrong. We all can work on becoming secure in our own points of view so that we do not become discombobulated by the opinions of others. You don't have to be right all the time. A difference of opinion doesn't necessarily mean you're wrong, either. It is also important to own our mistakes and apologize when necessary.

GROUP DISCUSSION: Think of a situation that made you feel disappointed because someone didn't see your point of view. Why do you think people feel insulted if others don't see things their way?
Facilitator, provide a personal response.

_____
_____
_____
_____

Review expectations.
When you take a good look at your expectations, you will get closer to the true understanding of the event. Perhaps your expectations were unrealistic. Maybe they could be adjusted a little to cope with your new reality. Either way, now is the time to question whether those expectations actually serve you.

GROUP DISCUSSION: Think of a situation when you were disappointed because your expectations were unrealistic. How can expectations be readjusted for a better result, and you still feel you haven't lowered your standards?

A Better Way: Real Talk with Real People

Facilitator, provide a personal response.

_____
_____
_____
_____

Facilitator, distribute comment cards, and have each class member write one thing they gained from this class.

A Better Way: Real Talk with Real People

Week 10 – Choices

1. Begin class with a discussion from Week 9 – Disappointment. Ask and allow a short question-answer period.

   Let's talk about choices. A choice is an act of making a decision when you have more than one possibility.
   GROUP DISCUSSION: If you could choose to be doing one thing in your life right now — other than being where you are — what would it be? Why? Facilitator, provide a personal response.

   _____
   _____
   _____

   We all wish we could go back and make a better choice at some point in our lives. Yesterday is gone. We can't change yesterday's choices, but we can change how we allow those choices to influence our decisions today. If we concentrated on the "coulda been" or "shoulda been," we'll miss opportunities for a better tomorrow.

   Have you ever wondered, *"How did I get myself into this mess?"* That 'mess' is the consequence of a choice you made. We all live with those types of outcomes. So, if your life isn't exactly what you thought it would be, take a look at some of the choices you have made along the way. If you don't want your life to continue on its current path, you are going to have to change your choices.

A Better Way: Real Talk with Real People

Where we are today is in direct correlation to the choices we've made. When we allow people, situations, or circumstances to influence our decisions, the consequences are often not what we want.

GROUP DISCUSSION: What are some of the consequences of a bad decision? How does it impact life?

Facilitator, provide a personal response.

_____
_____
_____
_____

The most straightforward decisions we make are the ones that are solely based on our own needs and wants. Those choices don't impact anyone else. However, more often than not, the choices we make are going to impact others. If we have children, spouses, family, and friends, we cannot make selfish decisions based on our own wants and needs. We must understand the impact.

Is that decision based on us yet hurts other people the correct choice? Or do we make a choice that benefits others and hurts us the wrong choice? Sometimes, we must sit and consider the consequences of making a decision that's in our best interest or the best interest of someone else.

GROUP DISCUSSION: Think of a decision you made that was in the best interest of someone else but not necessarily yourself. Why do you think people make decisions that are not in their best interest?

Facilitator, provide a personal response.

_____
_____
_____
_____

A Better Way: Real Talk with Real People

Have you ever stopped to think about the impact your choices have had or are having on your life? How often have you heard people say, "I have/had no choice"? Well, they had a choice; they just didn't like their options. It can be likened to a choice between the lesser of two evils, meaning they didn't particularly like either opportunity but had to choose one.

GROUP DISCUSSION: Think of a decision you had to make when you didn't like any of the choices. What's the best way to handle those situations? Facilitator, provide a personal response.

_____
_____
_____
_____

When we begin to take a careful look at the choices we make, it's easy to conclude that the most important choices are those that guide and direct the major areas of our lives. It's easy to think that if we make good choices about our career, marriage, education, family, income, etc., we should be able to do just fine. What about the other choices—the thousands of almost unnoticed choices we all make (or not make) day in and day out? How important are those little choices? They are essential! It may be the big choices in life that set the direction for where we're going, but it is the little ones that get us there.

So, what do some of those little choices look like? Let's take a look at some we make daily:

- What time am I going to get up?
- What am I going to wear today?
- What am I going to do today?

GROUP DISCUSSION: Think about life. What were some of the decisions you must make every day?
Facilitator, have participants give examples.

A Better Way: Real Talk with Real People

Decision-making is very personal. It's about determining what's best for you. Some of the decisions we make have nothing to do with someone else's best interest. Sometimes, our decisions can be self-destructive.

GROUP DISCUSSION: Think of a decision you've made that wasn't the best for you. What are some of the consequences made that aren't in the best interest of others?
Facilitator, provide a personal response.

_____
_____
_____
_____

Your choices should be your decision. You may consider someone else's opinion, but at the end of the day, what they see as important probably isn't the same thing you see. Everyone has their own agenda and is looking out for their best interest over yours. That doesn't necessarily mean that they intend you any harm, but you have to consider what whatever choice you make, you are the one who has to live with the consequences—whether good or bad.

GROUP DISCUSSION: What if you could back and change a decision you made that really impacted your life? How would you handle that situation were it to happen again?
Facilitator, provide a personal response.

_____
_____
_____
_____

A Better Way: Real Talk with Real People

Let's now look at situations that can cause bad decisions and the possible consequences that could come as a result:

a. **Not enough time** — those spur-of-the-moment decisions. Example: You volunteer to help someone, and you know you already have too much on your plate.
b. **Wallowing in chaos** — listening to others instead of that small voice inside your head. Example: Taking advice from someone about something that doesn't concern nor affects them.
c. **Avoiding the truth** — good decision-making is based on truth, whether it comes from you or is based on what someone is telling you. Example: You have a feeling your significant other is cheating on you, but you chose to ignore the signs. When someone tells you they saw him/her with someone else, you get mad at them instead of your mate.
d. **Procrastination/Fear** — some decisions are so complicated that we either don't want to make the wrong choice or we're just afraid. We feel if we don't make any decision, we can't make the wrong one. Unfortunately, what we don't understand is that when we don't make a decision, we've actually chosen the wrong one. Example: Your son has an accident in your car right after getting new insurance. You report it, then get afraid they were going to cancel. You decide not to return any calls or open any mail received from them. It turns out they do, indeed, cancel the insurance, but not because of the accident. They did so because they never received a response from you — a wrong choice.

No matter what you are faced with, making significant life decisions is never easy. In fact, it can be quite challenging. Sometimes, we get ourselves into situations where we feel we have no options or outlet for change. Prisons — whether self-imposed or actual incarceration — may seem like one of those situations. Still, you have a choice. You can choose to continue to live the life that you've been living or make a conscious choice to make better decisions this time around.

> **GROUP DISCUSSION:** What can be done so that you can make better decisions going forward with your life?

A Better Way: Real Talk with Real People

Facilitator, provide a personal response.

_____
_____
_____
_____

To help you make better decisions moving forward, let's look at a list of criteria you can use while making a choice. Facilitator, write on a whiteboard or easel (if available).

GROUP DISCUSSION: Consider the following when making a decision:

- What is important and valuable to you? What you value may not be of much importance to someone else, so know what you value most.
- Don't lose focus on your future. Many people tend to make choices based on life as it appears right now, instead of looking to the future. Does your choice and its ramifications stay within the goals that you have set for yourself for the future?
- Have you looked at all the alternatives and considered different scenarios? Sometimes, you just might consider a different outcome.
- How important is this decision? Are you willing to work on it? Don't get caught up with how important a choice is. Better yet, consider the positive impact it has on your life.
- Don't forget to use your intuition—your gut instinct—for your choices instead of your head.

Facilitator, distribute comment cards, and have each class member write one thing they gained from this class.

A Better Way: Real Talk with Real People
Week 11 – Dishonesty

1. Begin class with a discussion from Week 10 – Choices. Ask and allow a short question-answer period.

Types of lies:

- **Commission**
  If someone tells you something that is not a fact, that is a lie of commission. This type of lie is telling someone something that is simply not true. You're twisting the truth to create a (usually more favorable) version of something that happened.

- **Omission**
  Lying by omission is when a person leaves out essential information or fails to correct a pre-existing misconception in order to hide the truth from others. Lying by omission is not always intended to be harmful, as it is often thought of as an action undertaken to spare the recipient pain or embarrassment.

- **Influence**

  Sometimes, people will tell you something completely unrelated to the truth to cover up a lie. This is what we call a character lie or lie of influence. These lies are meant to make you believe the liar or to make the liar seem like such a great person, they are unlikely to be suspected of lying.

  GROUP DISCUSSION: If you could change one event in your past that was based on a lie, what would it be? Why?
  Facilitator, provide a personal response.

  _____
  _____
  _____
  _____

Truth vs. Lying

How many of you know people who lie, just to be lying? Some people get so accustomed to lying, they do so even when there is no apparent purpose. When their lies are easily disproven, they leave everyone else scratching their heads in wonder: What's the point of their deception? It just doesn't make any sense.

So, why do people tell lies? In a recent survey, the following were the suggested top six reasons why people lie:

1. **Control.** Unfortunately, control is the top reason why people lie. In an effort to control someone else's behavior, we will resort to dishonesty. Narcissists are often pathological liars because they simply don't care about the truth. They prefer to tell lies and gain control over people. Often, people tell lies because they are trying to control a situation and exert influence toward getting the decisions or reactions they want.
   GROUP DISCUSSION: Name a situation where you think someone lies to have control over another person. What do you think they're trying to control? Example: You tell your significant other what you know they want to hear.

A Better Way: Real Talk with Real People

Facilitator, provide a personal response.

_____
_____
_____
_____

2. **Impress.** In order to impress someone or to make a good impression, we will resort to lying. We might lie about who we are, what we have done, or where we are going. People who tell lie after lie are often worried about losing the respect of those around them. They want you to like them, be impressed by them, and value them. They're afraid the truth might lead you to reject or shame them.

   GROUP DISCUSSION: Name a situation where a person thinks they have to lie to impress someone. Why do you think they felt they had to lie? Example: You misrepresent yourself on a job application.
   Facilitator, provide a personal response.

   _____
   _____
   _____
   _____

3. **Vindictive.** Some people lie intentionally to cause harm to another person as a way of getting back at them. Often, they feel that person has harmed them. They tend to hold grudges and keep track of "pain points" against themselves to justify their actions. They will do whatever they can to challenge you, spread rumors about you, attack your reputation, or whatever else comes to mind.
   GROUP DISCUSSION: Name a situation where someone lies to hurt another person intentionally. Why do you think people tell vindictive lies?

A Better Way: Real Talk with Real People

Facilitator, provide a personal response.

_____
_____
_____
_____

4. **Defend/Protect.** One of the most common reasons for lying is to protect yourself. There might be a real consequence or a perceived one that a person is trying to defend themselves against. Some lies are told to protect others. In other cases, a lie is told to take on responsibility for things they are not responsible for to help someone else.
   GROUP DISCUSSION: Name a situation where a person might lie to either protect themselves or another. Why did they think they had to tell a lie? Facilitator, provide a personal response.

_____
_____
_____
_____

5. **Procrastination/Laziness.** When a person avoids their responsibilities, that's procrastination. The lie is more subtle in that the person knows they should be doing something but is intentionally putting it off. When we put off taking care of what needs to be done, we can easily convince ourselves that it isn't a big thing to get all worked up about. Then, the lie boils down to a person just being either lazy and not wanting to do the work, or they had no intention of doing the work in the first place, so they lie about it. If we're not careful, this mindset will take over and become how we handle (or not handle) our business. Eventually, people will stop believing anything we say we're going to do.
   GROUP DISCUSSION: Name a situation where someone might be dishonest either because they didn't want to do what was asked or they had no intention from the beginning on following through. How do you think that affected their relationship?

A Better Way: Real Talk with Real People

Facilitator, provide a personal response.

_____
_____
_____
_____

6. **Denial/Avoidance.** In this instance, the liar may want their lie to be true so badly, their desire and needs overwhelm their instinct to tell the truth. Sometimes, liars hope they can make something come true by saying it over and over or, at the very least, make it true if they believe it hard enough. We adjust our minds to "alternative facts" simply because we want to believe it.
   GROUP DISCUSSION: Name a situation where a person either believed a lie (even when they knew it wasn't true) or told a lie because they knew the other person wouldn't challenge the truth. What do you think the consequences of that lie might be?
   Facilitator, provide a personal example.

_____
_____
_____
_____

How does dishonesty affect relationships?

   a. **Lies erode trust.** Perhaps the most obvious impact that lying has on a relationship is the erosion of trust one person has in the other. Lies and trust cannot easily coexist. Eventually, the former will destroy the latter. Whether like a storm that causes a landslide, or rain that slowly eats away at a rock, lies can utterly change the landscape of a relationship and make it difficult — if not impossible — for one or both parties.
   Trust is essential for a healthy and successful relationship. When it is lost, the chances of a total collapse are astronomical.
   GROUP DISCUSSION: Name a situation where lack of trust might destroy a relationship. Why do you think trust is so important in a relationship?

A Better Way: Real Talk with Real People

Facilitator, provide a personal response.

_____
_____
_____
_____

b. **Lying shows a lack of respect.**
   Being told the truth—no matter what it may be—confers the feeling of respect upon the recipient. It proves to them that the other person places significant value upon the relationship and is not prepared to jeopardize it by being deceitful.
   While some truths will clearly put a relationship at risk, lies tend to be even more damaging. Telling someone the truth shows that you are willing to take responsibility for your actions. As soon as a lack of respect becomes apparent, it begins to put enormous strain on all aspects of the relationship and, if left unchecked, will destroy it altogether.
   GROUP DISCUSSION: Name a situation where you might feel totally disrespected because of a lie. How do you think that might affect the relationship?
   Facilitator, provide a personal response.

_____
_____
_____
_____

c. **Lying demonstrates selfishness.**
   When someone lies, their own self-interest is more important to them and comes before those of anyone else. More often than not, they will not make a sacrifice for the greater, long-term good of a relationship, much less for an immediate good. Unfortunately, this is another indicator that they do not place a high value on the person or relationship.

Selfish liars always have to have things their way and will lie to control every aspect of everything that happens, especially in their partner's life. Lies can also be an indication of more widespread selfishness and a disregard for anyone other than themselves.

GROUP DISCUSSION: Name a situation where someone might lie to get their way. What do you think the consequences of that lie would be? Facilitator, provide a personal response.

_____
_____
_____
_____

d. Waiting for the liar to slip up again.
Once you uncover a lie for the first time, it is almost impossible not to think of future untruths from that person. You begin to question what they are saying, passing their words through an internal alarm system in order to detect any hint of dishonesty. The problem is that having to be on constant alert for an inevitable lie puts a real strain on the interactions between the two. Sooner or later, the mental effort to decipher the truth from a lie will make the recipient want to avoid any conversation with the liar altogether. Also, knowing that if they lied once, they'd probably lie again is going to raise suspicion other times. The liar's reputation has been tarnished, and every move they make is questioned. Where are they? Who are they with? What are they doing? As a result, the relationship has become toxic.

GROUP DISCUSSION: Name a situation where you might begin to question everything the other person says. What can be done to change it? Facilitator, provide a personal response.

_____
_____
_____
_____

e. **Feeling like a fool for believing a lie.**
   That moment when you realize you've been lied to is a highly unpleasant one. When your eyes are opened to the truth, you can't help but feel foolish for even falling for the lie. At that point, you become angry at the other person for playing you for a fool, as well as angry at yourself for getting in that position.

   Being made to feel like a fool by another, especially someone you thought you could trust, eats away at all the positive feelings you may have towards them. The hurt may put up a wall between you, or it may cause old cracks to resurface and widen. Either way, your feelings for this person will be forever changed because of what they did to you and how they betrayed your trust.

   GROUP DISCUSSION: Name a situation where a lie from someone you trusted made you feel like a fool. What can be done to change that situation?

   Facilitator, provide a personal response.

   _____
   _____
   _____
   _____

f. **Lies beget lies.**
   We all know that one lie often leads to another…and another. To keep from getting caught, we will continue to build on the first lie until we often forget and lie about a previous lie. It becomes a vicious cycle. A habitual liar will see no real harm in telling "little white lies" to the people in their life.

   Unfortunately, where one lie might cause damage that can be mended in an otherwise strong relationship, multiple lies will serve to fan the flames of a fire that will eventually engulf any sense of cohesiveness that once existed. When lying becomes commonplace, no relationship can grow and survive.

   GROUP DISCUSSION: Think of a lie that causes people to have to continue lying to justify the first lie. How do you think this makes the person lied to feel?

A Better Way: Real Talk with Real People

Facilitator, provide a personal response.

_____
_____
_____
_____

Facilitator, distribute comment cards, and have each class member write one thing they gained from this class.

A Better Way: Real Talk with Real People
Week 12 – Goal Setting

1. Begin class with a discussion from Week 11 – Dishonesty. Ask and allow a short question-answer period.

2. It doesn't matter if you are going across town or the country, your journey begins with a destination and a map. Life is a journey. This final session is designed to give you the tools to determine a realistic goal and roadmap to get you there.
    GROUP DISCUSSION: If you could name a goal that you accomplished, what would it be? Why did you accomplish that goal and not others?
    Facilitator, provide a personal response.

    _____
    _____
    _____
    _____

A Better Way: Real Talk with Real People

3. **Why traditional goal setting doesn't work.**

   a. **We have too many goals.** Willpower is a force we all must deal with. Imagine willpower as the gas in your car. When you fill up your car, you have a certain amount of gas. The more you use your car, the more gas you use. It's the same with willpower. You use willpower every time you resist eating that temptation, build up the motivation to workout, or have that difficult conversation at work. Managing your willpower carefully and using it for the most critical goals in your life is a crucial factor in your success.

   By focusing on a few things that matter, you can better direct willpower towards building habits that will allow you to progress naturally in the direction of achievement, without having to stress. After all, forming habits might take some willpower, but eventually, they will become automatic. You can then reap the benefits without spending your precious stash of willpower. The better you are at focusing, the higher the rate of your success.

   GROUP DISCUSSION: Name some things in your life that require you to use willpower. Why are those things tempting to you? How do you resist the urge?

   Facilitator, provide a personal response.

   _____
   _____
   _____
   _____

   b. **We continually jump from one goal to another.** If we're not careful, we will find ourselves going from one thing to another, not accomplishing a single thing. That's like the internet. You can start out looking for one thing and, before you know it, you've clicked on multiple sites and find yourself in a rabbit hole.

   GROUP DISCUSSION: Name a time you had one goal, and before you accomplished that one, you jumped to another. What happened? Why did you switch your goals?

A Better Way: Real Talk with Real People

Facilitator, provide a personal response.

_____
_____
_____
_____

c. **It's hard to remember all of our goals.** As we age, our brains slowly lose the capacity to retain everything. If you've abused drugs or alcohol, you lost many brain cells along the way. They are gone forever. Get into the habit of writing down your goals!

   GROUP DISCUSSION: Think back and name something you wanted to accomplish that you've completely forgotten about. Was the goal important to you? Why do you think you forgot about it?

   Facilitator, provide a personal response.

_____
_____
_____
_____

d. **The enthusiasm and excitement for the goal wear off.** How many of us start the new year — every year — with New Year's resolutions? We're all excited for about two months...max. After that, the enthusiasm wears off, and we find ourselves spending less and less time focusing on those resolutions. Example: Going to the gym to work out and lose weight.

   GROUP DISCUSSION: Name something you said you were going to accomplish this year. How long did it take before you lost interest? Why do you think you lost interest?

   Facilitator, provide a personal response.

_____
_____
_____
_____

A Better Way: Real Talk with Real People

4. **From ideas to reality.**
    a. **Define your goals.** Are you setting financial, educational, health, or career goals? You must decide which area of your life you're going to work on first and then tackle the next. Although one goal may impact other areas of your life, defining only one goal cannot get you to where you want to be in all aspects of life.
    GROUP DISCUSSION: Name one goal you'd like to accomplish in each of the aforementioned areas. Which one would you like to work on first? Why?
    Facilitator, provide a personal response.

    _____
    _____
    _____
    _____

    b. **Confirm your commitment.** When you confirm your commitment, you're making a promise to yourself that you are going to do something. It means holding yourself accountable and writing down actionable steps that you can follow daily/weekly. It's best to make that same commitment to someone else who can hold you accountable.
    GROUP DISCUSSION: How committed are you to accomplishing your goals? Write down at least one step you are committed to doing weekly. How will it help you accomplish the goal?
    Facilitator, provide a personal response.

    _____
    _____
    _____
    _____

    c. **Overcome obstacles.** Everything in life you want to accomplish comes with obstacles. Often, we give up because we hit a stumbling block we didn't plan on, and we get knocked off-track. In order to overcome obstacles, you must have a plan in place.

A Better Way: Real Talk with Real People

GROUP DISCUSSION: Think of a goal you want to accomplish. What do you need to do to accomplish the goal? What would prevent you from reaching completion?

Facilitator, provide a personal response.

_____
_____
_____
_____

d. **S.M.A.R.T. Goals**
   i. Set **SPECIFIC** goals. Your goal must be clear and well-defined. A specific goal is one that incorporates an action plan that outlines how you will achieve the goal and a performance measure that tells you whether you were successful or not. Example: Stop smoking in six months.

   GROUP DISCUSSION: Name one specific goal to set for yourself. Why is this goal important to you?

   Facilitator, provide a personal response.

   _____
   _____
   _____
   _____

   ii. Set **MEASURABLE** goals. Include precise amounts, dates, and so on for your goals so that you can measure your degree of success. It means breaking down your goal into measurable elements.

   GROUP DISCUSSION: Break down the goal you specified into measurable elements. What is the first step you need to take to start working on your goal (i.e., stop smoking after meals or when bored, etc.)?

A Better Way: Real Talk with Real People

Facilitator, provide a personal response.

_____
_____
_____
_____

iii. Set **ATTAINABLE** goals. Make sure it's possible to achieve the goals you set. Goals must be achievable. The best goals require you to stretch a bit to achieve them, but they are not impossible to achieve.
GROUP DISCUSSION: Name a goal that you feel is impossible for you to achieve. Why can't you achieve the goal (i.e., setting a goal to win a 5K race when you don't exercise or run daily)?
Facilitator, provide a personal response.

_____
_____
_____
_____

iv. Set **RELEVANT** goals. Having the same goal as everyone else means you have others' goals. When setting a goal, ask yourself, "What does this goal mean to me?" Goals need to be realistic.
GROUP DISCUSSION: Think of a goal you set for yourself that was more important to someone else other than yourself. Why was that goal not so meaningful to you?
Facilitator, provide a personal response.

_____
_____
_____
_____

v. Set **TIME-BOUND** goals. The time-bound aspect of a goal enables the tracking of progress. Break down a goal into chunks of work that can be completed over time.

GROUP DISCUSSION: Think of a goal you set. Did you set a completion date? Why is the completion date important?

Facilitator, provide a personal response.

_____
_____
_____
_____

Facilitator, distribute comment cards, and have each class member write one thing they gained from this class.

www.ingramcontent.com/pod-product-compliance
Lightning Source LLC
Chambersburg PA
CBHW041536220426
43663CB00002B/56